Botswana

Botswana

BY SARA LOUISE KRAS

Enchantment of the World
Second Series

Children's Press®

A Division of Scholastic Inc.

NEW YORK   TORONTO   LONDON   AUCKLAND   SYDNEY
MEXICO CITY   NEW DELHI   HONG KONG
DANBURY, CONNECTICUT

Frontispiece: Basket weaver

Consultant: Brian Mokopakgosi, University of Botswana, Gabarone

Please note: All statistics are as up-to-date as possible at the time of publication.

Book production by Herman Adler

Library of Congress Cataloging-in-Publication Data

Kras, Sara Louise.
 Botswana / by Sara Louise Kras.
   p. cm.—(Enchantment of the world. Second series)
 Includes bibliographical references and index.
 ISBN-13: 978-0-516-24874-5
 ISBN-10: 0-516-24874-X
 1. Botswana—Juvenile literature. I. Title.
 DT2437.K73 2008
 968.83—dc22   2006102489

Botswana

Contents

Cover photo:
Elephants at a
water hole

Moremi Game Reserve

A young boy

The Gem of Africa

LYING IN THE SOUTHERN HEART OF AFRICA IS ONE OF the continent's success stories, the nation of Botswana. Although the British gained control of Botswana in the nineteenth century, they never ruled it directly. The people of Botswana come from many different ethnic groups. Most are Batswana, but there are also Kalanga, Hambukushu, Subiya, Birwa, Tswapong, San, and others. Yet once Botswana became independent, the country never broke down into warring groups as happened in many places. The people all consider themselves part of Botswana.

Opposite: **A woman of the Herero ethnic group wears a long, colorful dress.**

People in rural Botswana sometimes carry heavy loads on their heads.

Hundreds of years ago, the people that resided in the area that is now Botswana lived in scattered villages. They followed the rhythm of rural life, which included farming and tending cattle. The region's leaders relied on their ancient traditions. One of these traditions was having a *kgosi*, or chief, who ruled the tribe or village. Long ago, animals such as zebras, giraffes, elephants, lions, leopards, and warthogs roamed free. The *dik-gosi* (the plural of *kgosi*) were in charge of the animals. They carefully controlled how much wildlife was hunted. Tribal decisions were made in the *kgotla*, or meeting place. In the kgotla, tribespeople could speak about issues that concerned them.

Mosadi Seboko is the leader of the Balete people in Botswana. She is one of the highest-ranking female traditional leaders in all of Africa.

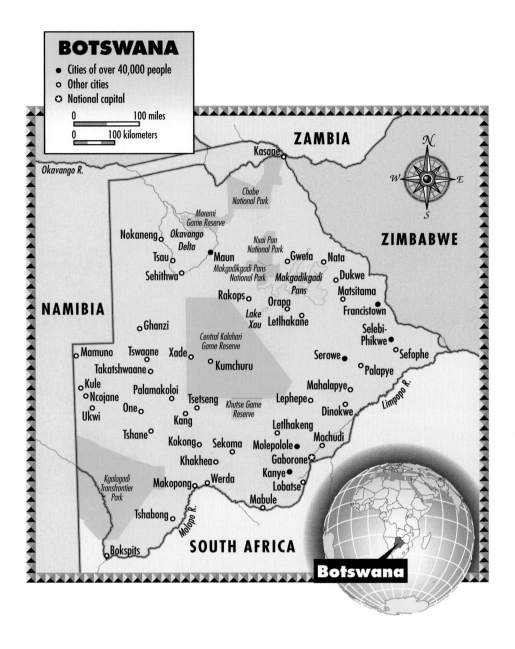

BOTSWANA

- • Cities of over 40,000 people
- ○ Other cities
- ✪ National capital

| 0 | 100 miles |
| 0 | 100 kilometers |

ZAMBIA

Okavango R.

Kasane

ZIMBABWE

Chobe National Park

Moremi Game Reserve

Nokaneng

Okavango Delta

Nxai Pan National Park

Tsau

Maun

Gweta

Nata

Sehithwa

Makgadikgadi Pans National Park

Makgadikgadi Pans

Dukwe

Matsitama

Rakops

Orapa

Francistown

NAMIBIA

Lake Xau

Letlhakane

Selebi-Phikwe

Ghanzi

Central Kalahari Game Reserve

Sefophe

Mamuno

Tswaane

Xade

Serowe

Palapye

Takatshwaane

Kumchuru

Kule

Mahalapye

Ncojane

Palamakoloi

Lephepe

One

Tsetseng

Khutse Game Reserve

Dinokwe

Limpopo R.

Ukwi

Kang

Letlhakeng

Tshane

Mochudi

Kokong

Sekoma

Molepolole

Gaborone

Khakhea

Kanye

Kgalagadi Transfrontier Park

Makopong

Werda

Lobatse

Mabule

Molopo R.

Tshabong

SOUTH AFRICA

Bokspits

Botswana

Today, many of the ancient traditions continue. The kgotla is the still the center of the village, and it is still headed by the kgosi. Discussions today also include modern issues, such as how to fight AIDS, a deadly disease that has ravaged Botswana.

Trucks haul away rock at the Jwaneng diamond mine. It is the richest diamond mine in the world.

After Botswana became independent in 1966, huge diamond reserves were found in the Kalahari Desert. This discovery transformed Botswana from a farming country into one of the largest diamond producers in the world. The Botswana government worked in partnership with the De Beers Mining Company of South Africa to reap the rewards of this valuable find.

Botswana has blossomed in recent decades. Today, modern buildings soar into the sky in the capital city, Gaborone. Businesspeople walk to and from work. Huge shopping malls sell clothes, beds, and hamburgers. The country's many paved roads make it easy to get around.

The government of Botswana recognizes that animals are one of the country's most valuable natural resources. The national government and village dikgosi have worked together to establish wildlife management areas. Because of this cooperation, the wildlife of Botswana is thriving. Tourists come from all over the world to see elephants feeding along the Chobe River and giraffes grazing in the Moremi Game Reserve. These sights make Botswana truly the gem of Africa.

More than a million people a year visit Botswana to see elephants and other wildlife.

From Desert to Delta

Wildebeests graze in Moremi Game Reserve in nothern Botswana.

Botswana lies in the middle of southern Africa, far from any ocean. Namibia is to the west and the north, Zambia to the north, Zimbabwe to the northeast, and South Africa to the southeast and the south.

Botswana is about the size of the state of Texas. It sits on a plateau—high, relatively flat land—yet it is surprisingly diverse. The Kalahari Desert stretches across central and southwestern Botswana. Northern Botswana is lush and green with thick forests. Eastern Botswana, where the land is the most fertile, is where most of the people live.

Opposite: **Flowers brighten the Kalahari Desert after a rain.**

The majestic Kalahari lion has a black mane. The creature can grow up to 10 feet (3 m) long.

The Kalahari Desert

Once called "Thirstland," the vast Kalahari Desert covers much of Botswana, along with parts of Namibia and South Africa. Scientifically, a desert is a region that receives less than 10 inches (25 centimeters) of rain per year. More rain than that falls in much of the Kalahari, so it is not a true desert. Most people call it a desert, however, because it is dry and sandy. The Kalahari is peppered with low bushes, thorny trees, and grass. In the southwest are huge rolling sand dunes where little plant life can take root.

Though water is scarce in the Kalahari, many animals make their home there, including the Kalahari lion, which has a thick black mane. The Kalahari is also home to hyenas, African wild cats, antelopes, ostriches, and a variety of small reptiles.

The Kalahari Desert has a rainy season and a dry season. The rainy season is from November to March, and the dry season is from May to August. When rain does fall, it comes heavy and fast, often flooding roads. During this time, grasses and shrubs grow rapidly, providing good grazing areas. Animals migrate to the Kalahari in huge numbers during the rainy season. In the dry season, the Kalahari is hot and dusty. The animals that stay in the region gather around shrinking water holes.

Lions drink water every day if they can. In dry times, they often go days without drinking, instead getting hydrated from their food.

Makgadikgadi Pans National Park lies in the northern Kalahari. This vast basin was once an ancient sea. Now, during the dry season, the parched ground curls into sections of salty, crunchy sand. The pans seem devoid of life then. In the rainy season, everything changes. The entire area fills with water.

Botswana's Geographic Features

Area: 224,607 square miles (581,730 sq km)

Largest Lake: Lake Ngami 40 miles (64 km) long and 4 to 8 miles (6 to 13 km) wide in the rainy season

Lowest Elevation: The confluence of the Shashe and Limpopo rivers, 1,684 feet (513 m)

Highest Elevation: Otse Mountain, 4,886 feet (1,489 m)

Greatest Distance North to South: 625 miles (1,006 km)

Greatest Distance East to West: 590 miles (950 km)

Longest Shared Border: South Africa, 1,143 miles (1,840 km)

Highest Average Temperature: 100°F (38°C) in January

Lowest Average Temperature: 32°F (0°C) in July

Highest Annual Rainfall: 25 inches (64 cm), in the north

Lowest Annual Rainfall: 5 inches (13 cm), in the west

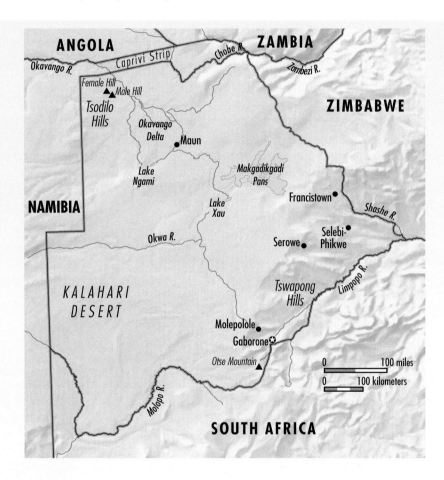

Wildebeests and zebras migrate to the Makgadikgadi Pans in incredible numbers. Peach-pink flamingos also head for the water, filling the sky as they fly in.

The Makgadikgadi is one of the largest salt pans in the world. It is nearly the size of the state of Indiana.

Kubu Island

The Makgadikgadi Pans are dotted with rock islands that rise above the ancient seabed. The most famous is Kubu Island, which rises about 60 feet (20 m) above the surrounding pan.

Kubu island is a magical place. Huge baobab trees seem to sprout out of the smooth rock. In the moonlight, the surrounding pans take on an eerie,

otherworldly glow. At sunrise, the rocks on Kubu Island turn pinkish, as the Sun's rays shoot out from behind feathery clouds.

The island bears evidence of ancient peoples. Parts of a low, circular stone wall can be seen. Ancient cutting tools and scraps of pottery dating back two thousand years have also been found there.

Okavango Delta

In northern Botswana is the Okavango River delta. A delta is land formed by the deposit of sand and soil at the mouth of a large river. The Okavango River flows into Botswana from Namibia. In Botswana, it becomes many streams, lakes, and lagoons. These wetlands are part of the Okavango Delta. Most river deltas end where they meet a larger body of water, but the Okavango ends in an area completely surrounded by land.

The Okavango is the largest inland delta in the world. With an area of about 6,600 square miles (17,000 square kilometers), it is slightly smaller than the state of New Jersey. The delta is a maze of palm-covered islands and water channels lined with papyrus reeds. In many areas, elephants and hippopotamuses have flattened the papyrus to make their way to the water.

The water in the Okavango River delta is unusually clean because few people live along the river's route from Angola to Botswana.

The delta is home to a huge variety of animals. Besides hippos and elephants, there are crocodiles, water buffalos, lions, giraffes, baboons, and many types of antelope. The delta also attracts hundreds of kinds of birds, such the anhinga, the masked weaver, the yellow-billed stork, and the wattled crane. During the dry season, tourists flock to the Okavango Delta to see the wildlife. At that time, many water holes have dried up, leaving the animals to gather around the few that remain. This makes it easier for people to spot them.

Baboons are among the many creatures that live in Okavango Delta. They feed on grass, seeds, berries, insects, and roots.

Botswana is located in the Southern Hemisphere, so the seasons there are the opposite of what they are in North America. Summer begins in October and ends in April. January is the hottest month, with temperatures sometimes reaching 100 degrees Fahrenheit (38 degrees Celsius). Winds and thunderstorms that blow in from the northeast cool many summer days.

Cape buffalos thunder across the Okavango Delta. These powerful creatures can defend themselves against most predators, including lions.

The winter months are from May to September. Winter days are warm, but at night temperatures can drop to as low as 32°F (0°C). Sometimes frost covers the ground. Little rain falls during the winter, and many water sources dry up. The exception is in the north, in the Okavango Delta and along the Chobe River. During the dry season, huge herds of wildlife journey to these areas.

As a whole, Botswana is generally dry. The average yearly rainfall in eastern Botswana is about 22 inches (56 cm). Parts of the west receive only about 5 inches (13 cm). The country has sometimes suffered devastating droughts. Rain is so important to the people of Botswana that the name for the nation's currency, the *pula*, means "rain."

Cities and Villages of Botswana

The capital, Gaborone, is the largest city in Botswana, with an estimated population of 186,007 in 2001. The second-largest city in Botswana is Francistown. It is located in the northeast and in 2001 had a population of 83,023. Francistown is one of the oldest towns in Botswana. It began as southern Africa's first gold-rush town when gold was discovered in 1867. Today, Francistown's frontier feel is gone. Instead, the town is abuzz with hotels, casinos, and nightclubs.

Molepolole is Botswana's third-largest settlement and largest village, with a population of 54,561. The term *village* dates back to the British era in Botswana. At that time, the British called traditional settlements "villages" and settlements founded by whites "towns." The British did not provide the same kind of services in villages that they did in towns. Molepolole is the village of the Bakwena people, one of the main subgroups of the Batswana. One of Botswana's oldest museums is in Molepolole. The Kgosi Sechele I Museum is named for the man who led the Bakwena from 1833 to 1892. The museum was founded to help preserve the region's culture. It displays traditional huts and provides information about birth, death, and marriage practices.

Selebi-Phikwe, the nation's fourth-largest city, with a population of 49,849, is a mining center in the east. Maun (left), the fifth-largest city, is a popular gateway for tourists visiting the Okavango Delta. It is often called the tourism capital of Botswana. Originally, this dusty village served as the capital of the Batawana tribe. Today, it is a hub of activity where 43,776 people live. Maun Airport is one of the busiest airports in southern Africa.

Serowe (below), the sixth-largest city in Botswana, had a population of 42,444 in 2001. It is the seat of the Bangwato people, who have produced some of Botswana's most famous statesmen. The first president of Botswana, Seretse Khama, came from the Bangwato.

Magnificent Life

T HE PEOPLE OF BOTSWANA TAKE GREAT PRIDE IN THEIR nation's abundant wildlife. Botswana is a natural animal paradise, one of the last on the entire continent of Africa.

Opposite: **Lions sleep as much as twenty hours a day.**

Wild Animals

Botswana is home to 164 species of mammals. These include the porcupine, Cape buffalo, vervet monkey, mongoose, jackal, spring hare, hippopotamus, and rhinoceros. A variety of big cats also calls Botswana home, such as lions, leopards, and cheetahs. The nation's hoofed animals include the kudu, impala, duiker, steenbok, waterbuck, wildebeest, eland, zebra, and giraffe.

Cheetahs are the speediest mammal on Earth. They are able to reach 70 miles (110 km) per hour over short distances.

The gemsbok is a desert antelope that thrives in the Kalahari Desert. It has adapted to extreme temperatures and can survive for days without water. This elegant antelope is slightly smaller than a horse, measuring about 4 feet (1.2 meters) tall at its shoulder. Though most of its body is light brown, it is trimmed with black and white on its head, belly, legs, and tail. The gemsbok's head is crowned with long, thin horns that can reach lengths of more than 3 feet (90 cm).

The red lechwe antelope is found in the Okavango Delta. The lechwe easily runs through mud and water because the bottoms of its hooves spread out. It is also an excellent swimmer.

Gemsboks mainly eat grass. If they can find no grass, they will dig to find roots.

Hippopotamuses are common in the Okavango Delta and along the Chobe River. These gigantic creatures can grow up to 13 feet (4 m) long and weigh more than 7,000 pounds (3,000 kilograms). Their tusks are sometimes 27 inches (70 cm) long. Though hippos look ungainly, they can run faster than people!

Hippos are vegetarians. They spend most of the day in the water, and then at night they head onto land, where they eat huge amounts of grass. They sometimes eat for six hours straight, consuming as much as 100 pounds (45 kg) of grass.

The hippopotamus is the most dangerous animal in Africa. It kills more people than all other types of animals put together. Hippos watch carefully over their territory. They will yawn to try to frighten off anyone or anything who comes near.

Hippopotamuses are the third-largest land animal. Only elephants and rhinoceroses are larger.

The black rhinoceroses is one of the world's most endangered animals. There are about three thousand left in Africa.

If the intruder does not retreat, the hippo attacks. Its tusks are razor sharp, so most victims of hippo attacks die. Anyone who comes between a mother hippo and her baby is in particular danger. People in small boats are also at risk, because a hippo can easily overturn a boat or bite it in two.

Two types of rhinoceroses live in Botswana, the black rhino and the white rhino. The mouths of black and white rhinos are shaped differently. The black rhino has a pointed top lip that hangs over its lower lip. The white rhino has wide flat lips. The white rhino is not really white at all. Instead, it is gray. Its name came from the words *wyd* or *weit*, both meaning "wide" in Afrikaans, the language of the Dutch settlers of southern Africa. To the English, the name sounded like "white," so the "wide-lipped rhinoceros" became the "white rhinoceros." A male white rhino can weigh 5,000 pounds (2,300 kg) and grow to be 13 feet (4 m) long.

Khama Rhino Sanctuary Trust

In 1989, some residents of Serowe in east-central Botswana grew concerned about the declining rhino population. Four years later, 17 square miles (44 sq km) of land was set aside to create a rhino sanctuary.

The rhinos in nearby Chobe National Park had long suffered at the hands of poachers, people who hunt wildlife illegally. The park's few remaining rhinos were captured and taken to the rhino sanctuary. South Africa also donated eight rhinos to the sanctuary.

The sanctuary is a success. Today, thirty-three rhinos live there. In fact, three rhinos had to be sold because there was no room for them in the park. The sanctuary is also home to ostriches, African wild cats, greater kudus, and impalas.

Rhinos are among the most endangered species in Botswana. Their numbers have dwindled over the years because of illegal hunting. Today, a few remain in the Mokolodi Game Reserve outside Gaborone and in the Khama Rhino Sanctuary Trust north of Serowe.

Leopards are solitary animals. To protect their kill from others, they drag it into high tree branches.

Leopards are large, beautiful cats, which have orange and white fur and black spots. They live all across Botswana, from the dry Kalahari to the wetlands of the Okavango Delta. Leopards make their home wherever they can find cover in rocky hillsides, thick brush, or forests. Leopards are incredibly powerful. They drag dead animals the size of a small horse high

Can Satellites Help Endangered Animals?

Scientists can learn much from tracking endangered animals. They can study the animals' habits and learn where the animals face the greatest danger from poachers. But tracking animals can be quite a challenge. Today, some researchers are dealing with this problem by capturing animals, fitting them with Global Positioning System (GPS) collars, and then releasing them. The GPS collars give off a signal that is picked up by satellites orbiting Earth. The GPS system allows scientists to find an animal's exact location. In Botswana, cheetahs, African wild dogs, and lions are just some of the animals being tracked by satellite.

Yellow-billed storks live near the water. They feed on fish and other water creatures.

into the trees where they can safely eat them. Unlike lions, which live in groups of up to thirty, leopards live alone except when they are breeding.

Birds

More than five hundred species of birds call Botswana home. Some species live in Botswana year-round, while others visit seasonally. Many are notable for one reason or another. The yellow-billed hornbill has a huge bananalike beak. The long-tailed starling shimmers dark blue. The African fish eagle sometimes sits high in a tree eating a fish it has caught with its long talons. The grey lourie, a bird common in Botswana, is also known as the "go-away bird." It earned its nickname because it makes a noise that sounds like the words *go away*.

The Okavango Delta attracts waterbirds such as storks, herons, pelicans, and flamingos. With their long curved necks and sticklike legs, flamingos manage to look both gawky and elegant. Two types of flamingos migrate to Botswana, The larger of the two, the greater flamingo, grows to heights of 4.6 feet (1.4 m).

The ostrich can be found throughout Botswana. This enormous bird weighs up to 350 pounds (160 kg) and can grow 9 feet (2.7 m) tall. The ostrich cannot fly, but it is an extremely fast runner, racing at speeds of up to 40 miles per hour (65 kph).

Ostriches lay the largest eggs of any creature on Earth. The eggs measure about 6 inches (15 cm) long and 5 inches (13 cm) wide. Ostrich eggs are important to the San people of Botswana. Once the contents of the eggs are eaten, the shell

Ostriches have excellent hearing and eyesight. This helps them avoid attack from predators.

The National Bird

The national bird of Botswana is the lilac-breasted roller. These striking, medium-sized birds have a lilac-colored breast and bright blue wings. They live on grasslands or among scrubby trees and feed on insects.

Kori bustards tend to live in areas with short grass. This allows them to see the surrounding area.

is used as a container. It can be filled with water and carried on long journeys. A water-filled ostrich egg can also be buried and then dug up during times of drought.

The Kori bustard, perhaps the heaviest flying bird in the world, also lives in Botswana. This large bird spends much time walking slowly through the grasslands searching for seeds, lizards, and other snacks. Kori bustards prefer walking to flying, but they will take to the air if threatened.

Domestic Animals

Botswana is home to many types of domestic animals. Some people keep cats and dogs as pets. Chickens, goats, and sheep are often seen roaming through villages. Cattle are the most abundant domestic animal in Botswana. In fact, the nation has more cattle than people. In 2003, about 1,700,000 cattle were living in Botswana.

Beef export is big business, and the Botswana government takes it seriously. Since the 1960s, the government has been building fences that divide Botswana into huge sections. The fences were originally built to keep cattle away from wildlife, so the cattle would not catch diseases. The fences also sometimes protect cattle from attack by predators. But the fences have proven dangerous to wildlife. Some disrupt animals' natural migration patterns. They also prevent wildlife from reaching water holes during times of drought. The government, conservation groups, and farmers are working to find a way to protect both wildlife and domestic animals.

Predators such as lions pose a great threat to cattle. Here, workers prepare lanterns that they use to help protect the cattle at night.

The National Animal

The Burchell's zebra is the national animal of Botswana. The zebra is shaped like a horse, but smaller. It is striped black and white with a short, stiff mane. Zebras graze constantly. They generally stay within 20 miles (32 km) of a water hole. Zebras usually live in family groups of about six animals, though they sometimes travel together in herds. Their main predators are lions, leopards, hyenas, and cheetahs.

Reptiles

Many reptiles live in Botswana's dusty towns and arid flatlands. Geckos and other lizards are often seen scurrying along the ground or up building walls. A variety of dangerous snakes live in Botswana. The black mamba is the largest venomous snake in Africa. It grows to an average of 8 feet (2.5 m) long, but some reach 14 feet (4 m). The black mamba usually eats birds, rats, and other small creatures. It is the fastest snake in the world, and some say the most aggressive. Its bite can be deadly. An hour after being bitten, a person may experience drooping eyelids, mental confusion, and shortness of breath. Then, the victim will go into convulsions and eventually die.

The black mamba is gray. Its name comes from the color of the inside of its mouth.

Jumping spiders have good eyesight. They can accurately strike prey from more than forty times their own body length away.

The puff adder, another deadly snake, is widespread in Botswana. It comes out at dusk to prey on rodents, birds, snakes, and tortoises. When threatened, it swells up while making a hissing sound similar to a tire losing air. A puff adder bite is extremely painful and causes massive swelling around the bite.

Insects, Fish, and More

Botswana is alive with insects and other small creatures. Like most places, Botswana is home to thousands of insect species, including many types of dragonflies, stick bugs, and beetles.

Scorpions dart through the desert, while jumping spiders leap like grasshoppers. Jumping spiders, which are hairy like tarantulas, can jump more than forty times their own body length.

Most of the fish in Botswana are found in the Okavango Delta. People come from all over the world to catch the tiger fish, bream, African pike, catfish, and bass that live there.

Plant Life

Botswana's terrain is extremely varied and so is its plant life. More than three thousand plant species have been identified in Botswana. Botswanan trees include the acacia, marula, silver leaf, and baobab. The mopane, which is also known as the ironwood tree, has bright green leaves that are shaped like butterflies. These trees abound in the Okavango Delta and the Moremi Game Reserve.

The sausage tree grows in the Okavango Delta. Its fruit looks like huge sausages. Each sausage tree fruit can weigh up to 9 pounds (4 kg). Some people refuse to camp under a sausage tree for fear one of these giant fruits might fall and conk them on the head.

Edible Tree Worms

Mopane worms are found on the mopane tree. These worms are a local delicacy. People pluck the worms off the trees and squeeze their insides out. Then they dry the worms in the sun and eat them. These worms can also be roasted, boiled, or fried. Oil, onion, and tomato are sometimes added to give them more flavor. The worms are often served with mealie meale, a cornmeal mush. Though the worms taste bland, they are an important source of protein. In some hotels, huge bowls of them are served at a buffet.

The Baobab

The baobab is one of Africa's most famous trees. What sets the baobab apart from other trees is its massive trunk, which measures between 16 feet (5 m) and 30 feet (9 m) across depending on the amount of water stored in the tree's trunk. Because baobab trees are huge, people have sometimes used them as meeting places or for shelter. Some of these trees are three thousand years old!

The bark of the baobab is a shiny pinkish-gray color. Elephants love to eat the spongy tissue of the baobab's trunk. They have been known to destroy entire trees during the dry season when water is difficult to find. Monkeys and baboons eat baobab seeds. People use the trees' fruit and leaves to make drinks and medicine.

Many legends have grown up around the baobab. Some say that when baobab seeds are soaked in water, the water can be used to protect a person from crocodiles. Another legend says that after soaking baobab bark in water, a man can drink the water and become very strong.

In dry regions, edible plants are highly valued. The tsamma melon is thought to be the ancestor of the watermelon. Tsamma melons grow in the Kalahari Desert, with many fruit clinging to a single vine. They have a high water content, and both people and animals use them as a water source. The San people who live in the Kalahari eat almost every part of the tsamma melon. They eat the fruit inside raw or mix it with meat. They boil the skin and then eat it. They even eat the roots, after roasting them on a bed of hot coals.

Magnificent Life **39**

Going Home

The Central Kalahari Game Reserve lies in the sandy heart of Botswana. It covers more territory than the nation of Switzerland. Giraffes, hyenas, cheetahs, lions, wildebeests, and many other creatures survive on its arid plains and sand dunes.

Nomadic people called the San have made this area their home for thousands of years. The Central Kalahari Game Reserve was established in 1961 as a place for the San to maintain their traditional hunting and gathering lifestyle. Officials later claimed that the San were a danger to reserve wildlife. In the 1990s, the government began forcing the San off the reserve. The San protested because the nation's constitution guarantees them the right to live there. In 2006, the San won a long-running legal case. The Botswana High Court said that the government had no right to remove them from the reserve. Once again, the San will be able to live on their ancestral lands.

Protected Areas

The government of Botswana has set aside vast tracts of land as protected areas. Moremi Game Reserve in the green Okavango Delta covers floodplains, forests, and lagoons. Many types of animals live within the reserve, including leopards, baboons, and crocodiles. Thickly wooded Chobe National Park has one of the highest concentrations of animals in all of Africa. It was named for the Chobe River, which runs along its northern border. Chobe National Park is known for its huge elephant population, which currently numbers more than one hundred thousand. The Kgalagadi Transfrontier Park is split between Botswana and South Africa. The park's endless miles of arid land allow for the natural migration of gemsbok and other hoofed animals.

The government of Botswana realized early on that the huge herds of animals that roam the land were a national treasure. Officials wanted to promote tourism, but in a way that would not endanger the wildlife. The result was a policy that limits the number of visitors to protected areas and charges them high prices. This gives the government the money it needs to care for its national parks. It also cuts back on the human impact on the parks. The policy has worked well, and as the twenty-first century progresses, much of Botswana's wildlife is thriving.

Elephants and hartebeests graze in the Moremi Game Reserve. The reseve was established in 1963.

Becoming Botswana

People have lived in the area that is now Botswana for at least one hundred thousand years. The region's early hunters and gatherers lived in makeshift huts and moved from place to place. Wherever game migrated, they followed.

Opposite: **The San have lived in southern Africa for thousands of years.**

Botswana's Early Peoples

The San were living in southern Africa by 30,000 years ago. They, too, were hunter-gatherers. Between 2,000 and 2,500 years ago, people began herding cattle and sheep in northern Botswana. Pottery was also used by this time. By A.D. 190, iron smelting had begun in the Tswapong Hills in east-central Botswana. Farming settlements near the Okavango Delta were established by 550.

A San woman in the Tsodilo Hills

The Tsodilo Hills

In the northwest corner of Botswana in the Kalahari Desert lie the Tsodilo Hills. These four hills contain the highest concentration of rock art in the world. More than 4,500 rock paintings can be found in an area of just 4 square miles (10 sq km). Some of these paintings depict people or animals, while others show geometric patterns. Scientists estimate that most of the paintings are between one thousand and two thousand years old.

Other important discoveries have been made in the Tsodilo Hills. Ancient mines were uncovered there. Scientists have also found bone fishhooks along with evidence of the shoreline from an ancient lake.

The San people consider the Tsodilo Hills sacred, because they believe the hills are the resting place for the spirits of the dead. The San believe that no hunting should take place near the hills. If someone hunts near the hills, the gods will cause misfortune to befall them.

The Batswana migrated into what is now Botswana from the north between one thousand and two thousand years ago. They pushed the San out of eastern Botswana, where the land is wet and fertile. The Batswana soon established villages there, while the San moved south into the forbidding environment of the Kalahari Desert.

Between the eleventh and the seventeenth centuries, various Batswana chiefdoms emerged in Botswana. These groups were involved in cattle herding, farming, and hunting.

Time of Great Troubles

The early 1800s was a turbulent time in southern Africa. Shaka, the leader of the Zulu people in southeastern Africa, was gathering many tribes under his control. He demanded that other groups join his forces or die. People began leaving the area, fleeing to the west. At the same time, white settlers were moving into southeastern Africa. They were fighting the black chiefdoms, and the black chiefdoms were fighting each other. All of this unrest meant that a lot of people were on the move. Many were starving and would steal what food or cattle they found. The Batswana had to protect their territory from these various groups.

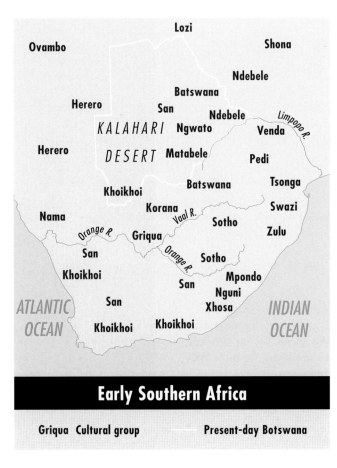

Early Southern Africa

Griqua Cultural group   ——— Present-day Botswana

Robert Moffat worked as a missionary for more than fifty years. During that time, he translated the Bible into Setswana.

During this terrible time, European missionaries began coming to Botswana. Some missionaries helped the Batswana organize to fight off the encroaching groups.

The London Missionary Society first sent people to southern Africa to preach Christianity in 1816. Robert Moffat was in charge of this group for fifty years. While in Botswana, Moffat set out to put Setswana, the language of the Batswana, into a written form.

David Livingstone arrived in 1841 to work with Moffat. He later married Moffat's daughter. Though Livingstone was a missionary, today he is better remembered for his explorations of southern Africa.

In 1852, Dutch South African colonists, who were known as Boers, began raiding the Botswana area. In time, the Batswana appealed to the British government for help in protecting themselves. On September 30, 1885, the British government made Botswana part of an area called the Bechuanaland Protectorate. Bechuanaland was technically not a colony as the British did not have direct rule and had promised Batswana self-rule. Rather, Bechuanaland was an area under British protection. The British policed the borders, preventing other colonial powers from gaining a foothold there.

Cecil Rhodes made a fortune mining diamonds in southern Africa. He cofounded the De Beers Mining Company, which at its peak controlled 90 percent of the world's diamonds.

The greatest threat to Bechuanaland's independence came from an Englishman named Cecil Rhodes. He was the powerful owner of the British South Africa Company (BSAC), a mining and trading company. Rhodes had a grand plan. He wanted to build a railroad all the way across Africa, from Cape Town in the south to Cairo in the north. Rhodes approached the British government with his plan, which

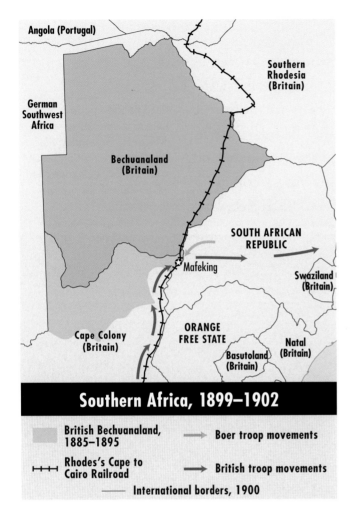

Southern Africa, 1899–1902

British Bechuanaland,
1885–1895

Rhodes's Cape to
Cairo Railroad

International borders, 1900

Boer troop movements

British troop movements

included putting Bechuanaland under his control in order to expand his mining operations.

To prevent Rhodes from taking over Bechuanaland, three leading tribal chiefs—Khama III, Bathoen I, and Sebele—traveled to England in 1895. There, the dikgosi met with the British colonial secretary. The result of their visit to England was a compromise. The British agreed that they would not turn over Bechuanaland to Rhodes, and the dikgosi granted Rhodes a narrow strip of land for his railway.

From 1895 to 1964, the British invested little in Bechuanaland. They thought of it as little more than a rail route. To raise money from this poor region, a "hut tax" was introduced in 1899. This was a tax that the people of Bechuanaland were supposed to pay on each hut a family had. Most people in the region thought the tax was unfair, and few had the money to pay it. Some men left their families to work in mines in South Africa in order to earn money to pay the tax. This development fueled the idea that Bechuanaland might one day become part of South Africa.

Toward Independence

The Bangwato tribe would be crucial in Bechuanaland's movement toward independence. In 1925, Seretse Khama, the grandson of Khama III, became kgosi of the Bangwato. The only problem was that he was just four years old. To handle this situation, his uncle, Tshekedi Khama, acted in Seretse's place and became regent. He would rule the Bangwato while Seretse Khama grew up.

Tshekedi Khama became a strong leader who stood up to the British authorities. In 1934, the British passed proclamations that limited the power of the dikgosi. Tshekedi Khama and another kgosi Bathoen II of the Bangwaketse, protested that these proclamations were not legal. They took the British high commissioner, the leading British official in the region, to court over these proclamations. Their efforts paid off. In 1943, new laws were passed that returned some powers to the dikgosi.

Tshekedi Khama (right) was the acting leader of the Bangwato for more than twenty years.

The marriage of Seretse Khama and Ruth Williams created a furor. They were shunned in southern Africa.

By 1944, Seretse Khama was old enough to rule the Bangwato. Instead of taking on the duties of kgosi, he went to England to study law. Tshekedi Khama continued ruling the Bangwato in Seretse's place. While in England, Seretse met a white Englishwoman, Ruth Williams. They fell in love and were married in 1948.

The white minority who controlled South Africa had just passed a group of laws that sorted people based on their race. In South Africa, the government identified people as black, white, or colored, which included both Asians and people of mixed descent. Your race determined where you could live, what job you could have, and what kind of education you would get. This policy was called *apartheid*, a word that means "separateness" in Afrikaans, the language of South Africa's white rulers.

Given this extreme racism, Seretse Khama's marriage created an uproar—in South Africa, in Bechuanaland, and in neighboring Rhodesia (now Zimbabwe). When Seretse returned to Bechuanaland, Tshekedi Khama and the British authorities rejected him. The British government had close economic ties to South Africa and Rhodesia. British officials wanted to remain friendly with the leaders of these nations, so they asked Seretse to return to England. When Seretse arrived in England in 1950, he was told he could not return to Bechuanaland.

Many Bangwato did not approve of Seretse's marriage. Still, they were angered by the way the British treated him. People took to the streets, demanding his return.

Seretse wanted to help his people. The only way he could do this was to be in Bechuanaland. But the British would not

The First President

Seretse Khama was born in 1921. At age four, he was named kgosi of the Bangwato people. Seretse was educated in South Africa and Great Britain. His marriage to a white Englishwoman forced him into exile in Britain. He returned to Bechuanaland as a private citizen and soon became involved in politics. He worked tirelessly for Bechuanaland's independence. His wisdom and patience would lead him to become the first president of Botswana.

allow him to return as long as he was kgosi of the Bangwato. So, in 1956, he renounced his title and returned home. He spent the next several years promoting Botswana's independence.

To the Present

Through the efforts of Seretse Khama, Tshekedi Khama, and other leaders, Bechuanaland was ripe for independence. National spirit ran high, and in 1961 a legislative council was elected. A proposal of democratic self-government in Bechuanaland was submitted to Britain in 1963. The following year, it was accepted.

By this time, two political parties had formed. Seretse Khama led the Bechuanaland Democratic Party (BDP), which was later called the Botswana Democratic Party. The other was the Bechuanaland People's Party (BPP), which was later called the Botswana People's Party. The BPP supported quick social change, including forcing all white settlers in the nation to leave. The BDP also wanted to achieve change, but it took a more cautious approach.

By 1965, Bechuanaland was moving rapidly toward independence. Elections were held, and the BDP won in a landslide. On September 30, 1966, the new Republic of Botswana gained complete independence with Seretse Khama named the first president. Seretse Khama remained popular, and he was reelected twice.

Seretse Khama died in 1980. His vice president, Ketumile Masire, assumed the presidency and was reelected in 1984.

Masire was a longtime ally of Seretse Khama, having cofounded the BDP back in the 1960s.

Botswana's economy grew quickly during the Masire presidency, but the nation also faced difficulties. South African troops raided Botswana several times, because Botswana was a member of the Front Line States. This organization had been established by southern African countries pushing for black rule in South Africa. South Africa conducted a raid into Botswana in 1985 in which fifteen civilians were killed. Apartheid finally came to an end in South Africa in the early 1990s, and the black majority population took control of the government there.

Masire was reelected president of Botswana in 1989 and 1994. In 1997, the National Assembly changed the constitution to prohibit a president from holding office for more than two terms. President Masire announced his retirement in 1998. His vice president, Festus Mogae, was then appointed president.

Botswana has been remarkably stable in its decades as an independent nation. Heading into the future, it seems ready to meet the challenges it faces.

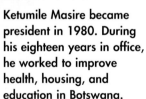

Ketumile Masire became president in 1980. During his eighteen years in office, he worked to improve health, housing, and education in Botswana.

A Democratic
Success

SINCE BECOMING INDEPENDENT, BOTSWANA HAS HELD free elections regularly. The nation is functioning well as a multiparty democracy. It is a democratic success story.

Opposite: **A solider leads a band during events celebrating Botswana's fortieth year of independence.**

The Constitution

Botswana's constitution was adopted on September 30, 1966. The constitution lays out the structure of the national government. Botswana's constitution divides the government into three branches: executive, legislative, and judicial. It also describes the functions of each branch.

The attorney general's sleek offices are in Gabarone.

The constitution guarantees the people of Botswana freedom of speech and the right to privacy. They are also guaranteed protection of the law regardless of color, religion, or sex. The constitution clearly states that slavery and forced labor are against the law. Torture and degrading punishment are also strictly forbidden. The death penalty is still allowed in Botswana.

Executive Branch

The executive branch is headed by the president. In general, the president's job is to provide leadership and ensure security for the people of Botswana. To become president, a person

The Botswana National Assembly meets in a low-slung building in Gaborone.

must be a citizen of Botswana and be at least thirty years old. The president is restricted to two five-year terms of office. He or she is elected by the members of the National Assembly.

The president governs with the assistance of a vice president and a cabinet. The cabinet consists of fifteen ministers who oversee different parts of the government. These ministers run sections such as the Ministry of Trade and Industry, the Ministry of Education, and the Ministry of Work and Transport. The cabinet ministers help the president make and apply policy.

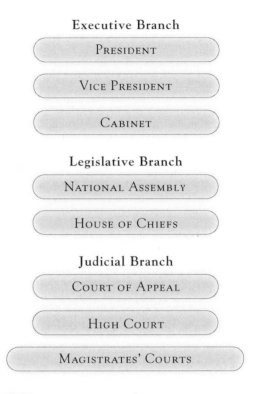

NATIONAL GOVERNMENT OF BOTSWANA

Executive Branch
PRESIDENT
VICE PRESIDENT
CABINET

Legislative Branch
NATIONAL ASSEMBLY
HOUSE OF CHIEFS

Judicial Branch
COURT OF APPEAL
HIGH COURT
MAGISTRATES' COURTS

Legislative Branch

The lawmaking branch of Botswana's government is called the National Assembly. The National Assembly has sixty-two members. Fifty-seven of them are elected by the people. Four are chosen by the party with the most seats in the National Assembly. The final member is the president.

Besides making laws, the National Assembly is also in charge of public funds. In addition, its members are responsible for ensuring that the government knows the will of the people and that Botswana's cultural heritage is preserved.

The Coat of Arms

Botswana's national coat of arms shows two zebras holding up a shield. The zebra on the left is holding an elephant tusk. The zebra on the right is supporting an ear of sorghum, an important crop in Botswana. The three cogwheels on the top of the shield represent industry. The three blue waves in the middle indicate the importance of water to Botswana. At the bottom of the shield is a bull's head, which represents the importance of the cattle industry. *Pula*, meaning "rain," is written on the banner along the bottom.

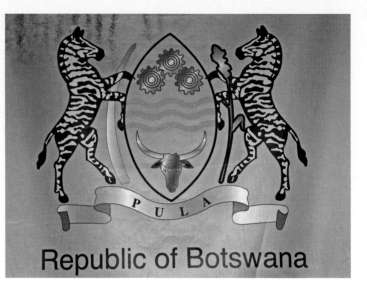

Governing in the Kgotla

A saying in Botswana goes, "The highest form of war is dialogue." This idea can be seen in the way many villages in Botswana continue to use the kgotla meeting. In the kgotla, people discuss issues openly. Disagreements are aired, and people learn tolerance for other viewpoints. This allows people to have a say in how problems are handled.

Marriages and divorces are performed in the kgotla. The kgosi also settles local judicial matters in the kgotla.

In the past, women were not allowed to speak in the kgotla. This is no longer the case. Some women have even become dikgosi. In rural Botswana, the kgosi is still considered the leader and direct representative of a tribe.

A second part of the legislative branch, the House of Chiefs (called the Ntlo ya Dikgosi in Setswana), dates back to the days when Botswana was a British protectorate. The House of Chiefs has no lawmaking powers. Instead, it advises other parts of government. Any bill having to do with tribal property, tribal organization, or customary law or courts must go through the House of Chiefs for discussion before it can be passed.

The House of Chiefs has thirty-three members. Eight of its members are the leaders of the groups that were self-governing prior to independence. Five are appointed by the president. The other twenty are chosen according to region.

A group of San wait to hear a High Court decision concerning whether they will be allowed to live in their traditional homeland.

Judicial Branch

The judicial branch oversees the law of the land. It is composed of the High Court, the Court of Appeal, and magistrates' courts. In addition, tribal customary courts deal with some local problems and some criminal matters. They have limited power.

The National Flag

The flag of Botswana is made of five horizontal stripes. The top and bottom are wide, light-blue stripes. They are separated from a middle black stripe by white stripes. The blue stripes represent sky and water. The black and white stripes symbolize Botswana's dedication to racial harmony. The stripes were inspired by the national animal, the zebra, which is part of Botswana's coat of arms.

The National Anthem

When Botswana became independent in 1966, it adopted an anthem written by K. T. Motsete. It is titled "Fatshe Leno La Rona" ("Blessed Be This Noble Land").

Setswana lyrics

Fatshe leno la rona,
Ke mpho ya Modimo,
Ke boswa jwa borraetsho;
A le nne ka kagiso.

CHORUS:
Tsogang, tsogang! banna, tsogang!
Emang, basadi, emang, tlhagafalang!
Re kopaneleng go direla
Lefatshe la rona.

Ina lentle la tumo
La chaba ya Botswana,
Ka kutlwano le kagisano,
E bopagantswe mmogo.

CHORUS

English lyrics

Blessed be this noble land,
Gift to us from God's strong hand,
Heritage our fathers left to us,
May it always be at peace

CHORUS:
Awake, awake! O men, awake!
And women close behind them stand!
Together we'll work and serve,
This land, this happy land.

Work of beauty and of fame,
The name Botswana to us came,
Through our unity and harmony,
We'll remain at peace as one.

CHORUS

All citizens of Botswana who are at least eighteen years old can vote. Elections for the National Assembly are held every five years.

The party that wins the most seats in the National Assembly forms the government. Several political parties compete for power in Botswana. The most successful has been the Botswana Democratic Party, which has held power continuously since independence.

Independence Day

Every September 30, people throughout Botswana celebrate Independence Day with much fanfare. The biggest celebration is in Gaborone. A huge fireworks display at the National Stadium kicks off the festivities on the eve of Independence Day. The next morning, throbbing music blares as trucks filled with people head toward the stadium.

The event begins with the military in full uniform marching in the center of the field. A car carrying the president then arrives and drives around the field. The president waves as the audience members clap, wave, and wail.

Children on one side of the stadium have large flip cards. When they all hold up their cards at once, it spells out a message or makes a colorful picture. The event also includes a traditional dance performance. The dancers wear leather skirts and tops and have rattles attached to their ankles.

A band plays "Happy Birthday" as airplanes fly overhead. Balloons are then released into the air. A few floats go by amid much cheering, and the Independence Day festivities come to an end.

Gaborone: Did You Know This?

Gaborone was established as Botswana's capital when the nation became independent on September 30, 1966. Before independence, the Botswana region's seat of government was in Mafikeng, in South Africa.

Gabrone is named after Kgosi Gaborone of the Batlokwa tribe. He led his people in the area of Gaborone in the 1880s.

Gaborone was chosen to be the capital because it already had administrative offices. It also had rail service and a good water source. Gaborone was considered a neutral city, where no one ethnic group held sway.

Gaborone is about 9 miles (15 km) from the South African border, in southeastern Botswana. In the 1960s, it was a small village, but after independence, it expanded quickly. Today, it is a bustling city of nearly two hundred thousand people. Apart from government buildings, it also has the National Museum and Art Gallery, the University of Botswana, and the headquarters of the national television service.

The National Stadium hosts soccer matches as well as trade fairs and cultural conventions. Music and drama performances are held regularly at the Maitisong Cultural Centre.

Outside Gaborone, a huge dam provides the city with a steady water supply. Two game reserves are nearby. The Gaborone Game Reserve opened in 1988. Visitors can see zebras, ostriches, kudus, and a variety of birds. At the Mokolodi Nature Reserve, they can catch glimpses of a wider variety of animals, including cheetahs, giraffes, elephants, leopards, and white rhinoceroses.

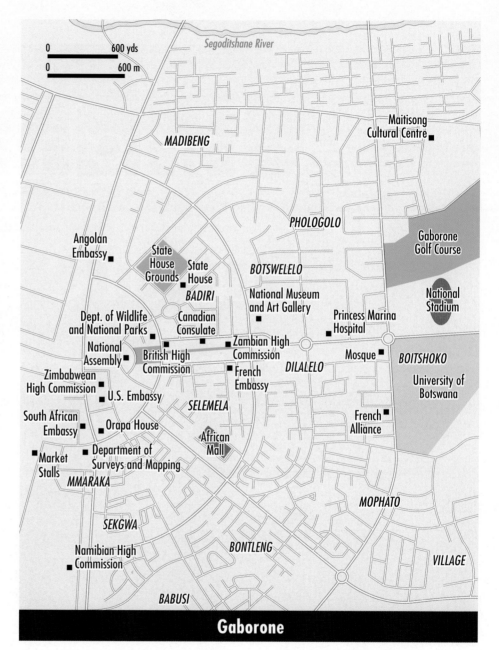

Gaborone

A Bright
Future

Diamond mining is vital to Botswana's economy.

BOTSWANA IS A POOR COUNTRY COMPARED WITH MANY countries in the West. Yet it is one of the wealthiest nations in southern Africa. More than 75 percent of its citizens are employed.

Much of Botswana is dry and barren, not suitable for agriculture. Yet the dry Kalahari Desert, once thought of as a wasteland, has yielded Botswana's largest profit. Diamonds were discovered there, and today Botswana is the largest diamond producer in the world.

Opposite: **Tourists travel in sturdy offroad trucks for safaris in the vast Kalahari Desert.**

Money Facts

In 1976, the pula became Botswana's national currency, replacing the South African rand. The pula is divided into 100 thebe. *Pula* means "rain," and *thebe* means "shield." Coins are worth 5, 10, 25, and 50 thebe and 1, 2, and 5 pula. Pula banknotes come in values of 10, 20, 50, and 100. In 2007, it took about 6 pula to equal to US$1. One pula was equal to about 17 U.S. cents.

Pula bills display images of leaders from Botswana's history and the nation's resources and wildlife. For example, the 50-pula note shows Seretse Khama, the first president of Botswana. The 100-pula note has a picture of a diamond mine. All pula bills display the national shield.

Tourism is Botswana's other main source of income. Tourists spend millions of dollars every year in Botswana. They stay in expensive lodges and camps to get a close-up view of Botswana's wildlife.

Botswana's Diamonds

Many stones and metals are mined in Botswana. The most profitable is diamonds. In 2005, diamonds accounted for more than 80 percent of Botswana's total export earnings. The nation exported almost US$3 billion worth of diamonds.

How Much Does It Cost?

	In Pula	In US$
1 loaf of bread	3.10	0.51
1 liter of milk	4.50	0.74
1 Coke	3.50	0.58
2 liters of ice cream	22.25	3.66
1 bag of carrots	3.25	0.53
1 bottle of ketchup	7.95	1.31
½ dozen eggs	4.30	0.71

A worker in Gabarone sorts diamonds unearthed at nearby mines.

The world's largest diamond producer is the Debswana Diamond Company. This company has two equal owners: the government of Botswana and De Beers Investments from South Africa. Diamond mining transformed Botswana's struggling agricultural economy into one of the fastest growing economies in the world.

The first diamond reserve in Botswana was discovered in 1967 by a team from De Beers who had been searching for twelve years. It was located near the village of Letlhakane in north-central Botswana. It became known as the Orapa mine. One of the richest diamond mines in the world was discovered in the 1970s in southeast Botswana in an area called Jwaneng.

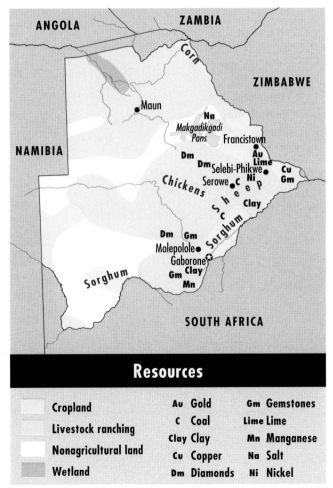

Resources

Map key		
Cropland	Au Gold	Gm Gemstones
Livestock ranching	C Coal	Lime Lime
Nonagricultural land	Clay Clay	Mn Manganese
	Cu Copper	Na Salt
Wetland	Dm Diamonds	Ni Nickel

It used to be that all rough diamond stones mined in Botswana were shipped overseas to be cut and polished. Today, most diamonds are cut and polished in Botswana.

Gold mining has recently become a source of income for Botswana. An Australian company began mining for gold around the Francistown area in 2004.

Tourism

Tourism is an essential part of Botswana's economy. In 2002, more than a million tourists traveled to Botswana and spent US$309 million. The main reason tourists go to Botswana is to see wildlife. Most tourists stay in tented camps. Visitors can choose among camps in the Okavango Delta, the Moremi Game Reserve, Chobe National Park, and even the Kalahari Desert.

People from all over the world travel to Botswana to get a close-up look at lions and other creatures.

A Typical Day in a Tented Camp

The day begins early in a tented camp. Tourists get up at 5:30 A.M. After coffee or tea and a snack, they pile into open jeeps to go on a game drive. The drive usually lasts for about two hours. During that time, they may see impalas, warthogs, giraffes, baboons, crocodiles, and perhaps a pride of lions.

Once the tourists arrive back at camp, they eat breakfast and then return to their tent for a shower and nap. At 3:30 P.M., the visitors have tea and then go on another two-hour game drive. When they return, they go back to their tents and clean up for dinner.

Tourists are not allowed to walk on their own in the evening for fear of encountering a wild animal such as a wandering hippo or elephant. Instead, at dinner time, a camp guide must come to their tent and accompany them with a flashlight to the dining hall. After dinner, guides lead the tourists back to the safety of their tents.

More cattle than people live on Botswana's grasslands.

Agriculture and Manufacturing

Raising cattle is the most important agricultural activity in Botswana. Most cattle are sold to the government-owned Botswana Meat Commission in Lobatse, a town 43 miles (69 km) southwest of Gaborone. It is the headquarters of the largest meat processing plant in Botswana.

The Lobatse facility is a slaughterhouse, a canning service, and a tanning plant, where hides are turned into leather. The facility can handle 800 cattle and 500 smaller livestock per day. Another slaughterhouse, in Francistown, can handle 400 cattle and 150 smaller livestock per day. Much of the beef is exported to other African nations or Europe.

Farmers in Botswana also grow crops to feed their families or to sell locally. These crops include potatoes, beans, corn, millet, and sorghum. During droughts, crops are sometimes not adequate to feed the population. Then, basic food items must be imported so that people do not starve.

Manufacturing plays only a small role in Botswana's economy. Bottled beer, soft drinks, and textiles are some of the products made in Botswana.

Imports and Exports

In recent years, Botswana's exports to other countries have had a higher value than its imports from other countries. This indicates a strong economy. Some of Botswana's main imported items are food, beverages, and tobacco. The country also imports

What Botswana Grows, Makes, and Mines

Agriculture (2003)

Roots and tubers	93,000 metric tons
Sorghum	32,000 metric tons
Peas, beans, and lentils	19,000 metric tons

Manufacturing

Livestock products (2003)	168,000 metric tons
Beer (2001)	1,692,000 hectoliters
Soft drinks (2001)	431,000 hectoliters

Mining (2002)

Crushed stone	3,602,257 metric tons
Hard coal	953,081 metric tons
Salt	315,259 metric tons

chemicals, rubber, wood, paper products, machinery, electrical equipment, and cars. Botswana's most valuable export by far is diamonds. It also exports metal products and meat.

Botswana's major trading partners are other southern African nations such as Lesotho, South Africa, Namibia, Swaziland, and Zimbabwe. Botswana also trades with the United States, South Korea, and the United Kingdom.

About half the people in Botswana have cell phones.

Communications

Cellular phones are popular in Botswana. In 2005, 823,100 people in Botswana had cell phones. In all of Africa, Botswana's rate of cell phone ownership is second only to South Africa's.

Computers are becoming more common in Botswana. Many businesses and government agencies now have Web sites, and more than one hundred thousand computers are in use.

Botswana's largest newspaper, an English-language paper called the *Daily News*, is published on weekdays. It is also published in Setswana under the name *Dikgang tsa Gompieno*. Another paper, called the *Mmegi Monitor,* is published Mondays. Other newspapers include the *Voice, Mmegi wa Dikgang,* the *Echo,* and the *Ngami Times.*

Botswana has two government-operated radio stations, Radio Botswana 1 and Radio Botswana 2. During Radio Botswana 1's broadcast, it's not unusual to hear a ringing cowbell, the national anthem, and prayers. The station broadcasts both cultural programs and news shows. Both English and Setswana are spoken on Radio Botswana 1.

Radio Botswana 2 is Botswana's first commercial radio channel. The people behind Radio Botswana 2 are trying to attract an audience between the ages of fifteen and forty-five. The programming is mainly in English. Botswana also has two privately run radio stations, Yarona FM and Gabz FM, which play pop music.

Botswana Television went on the air in 2000. During the week, it delivers eight hours of local and international programming. On the weekend, it broadcasts for ten hours. Sixty percent of its programs deal with local subject matter. Satellite TV from South Africa, which offers about fifty-five channels, is also available in Botswana.

Electricity

In rural parts of Botswana, people pay for their electricity before they use it by buying tokens or a card. If a family runs out of prepaid electricity, they must buy more for the electricity to come back on.

The Botswana countryside has many well-maintained roads.

Botswana gets its electricity from the Morupule power station, outside of Palapye, which uses locally mined coal. If there is a power shortage, electricity is imported, usually from South Africa. Plans are in the works to expand the Morupule station and build a second one. Once these projects are completed, Botswana will have more power than it needs and will likely export power to nearby countries.

Transportation

When Botswana first became independent, it had about 5 miles (8 km) of paved roads. Driving short distances could take many hours because of the rough roads. The government quickly got to work, and today Botswana has more than 15,000 miles (24,000 km) of road. About 5,500 miles (8,900 km) of these are well-maintained paved roads.

In most parts of the country, there are few cars, and traffic is light. In Gaborone, however, traffic has become a problem during rush hour.

Botswana Railways has a train track running across the country for 552 miles (888 km). It is mainly used for transporting freight from the Selebi-Phikwe copper and nickel mine, coal from Morupule, and soda ash from the Sua Pan. Two passenger routes run from Gaborone to Francistown and from Lobatse to Bulawayo in Zimbabwe.

Air Botswana serves all major cities of Botswana. It also flies to Cape Town and Johannesburg in South Africa and to Harare, Zimbabwe. The main international airport in Botswana is the Sir Seretse Khama airport in Gaborone. In addition, the Maun, Francistown, Kasane, and Ghanzi airports are frequently used. More than a hundred airfields are scattered through the country, mostly near camps and lodges.

Weights and Measurements

Botswana uses the metric system, which includes units such as meters and kilograms. One meter is equal to 39 inches, and 1 kilogram is about 2.2 pounds.

Maun Airport, in northern Botswana, is the country's main tourist airport. Most visitors to the Okavango Delta arrive in Maun.

Living Together

Opposite: **About 36 percent of the people in Botswana are under fifteen years old.**

Many countries across the globe have seen wars between ethnic groups. The story of Botswana is different. After the country gained complete independence, it never broke down into warring factions. The first president of Botswana, Seretse Khama, promoted unity among all the citizens of Botswana, regardless of their ethnic group. The people of Botswana continue to strive for this ideal today.

Most people in Botswana live in towns or villages.

Population of Botswana's Largest Cities and Villages (2001 est.)	
Gaborone	186,007
Francistown	83,023
Molepolole	54,561
Selebi-Phikwe	49,849
Maun	43,776
Serowe	42,444

In 2006, an estimated 1,639,833 people lived in Botswana. It is a young country. Between 60 and 70 percent of the people are under thirty years old.

Many people in Botswana live in rural areas, usually in villages. They farm and take care of their livestock. Living in the city is becoming more common, however. Today, slightly more than half the people in Botswana live in urban areas.

Rural men fish in the Okavango Delta.

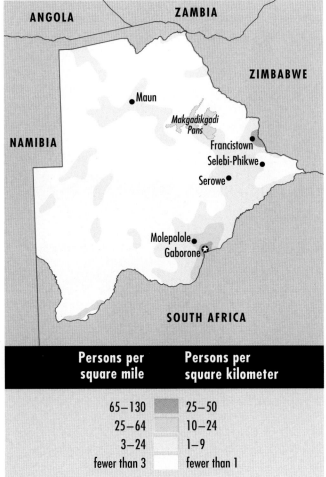

Persons per square mile		Persons per square kilometer	
65–130		25–50	
25–64		10–24	
3–24		1–9	
fewer than 3		fewer than 1	

Like ranchers around the world, those in Botswana must drive their cattle between grazing areas, slaughterhouses, and markets. These men have just completed a 300-mile (500 km) drive across the Kalahari.

The Batswana

About 70 percent of the people in Botswana are Batswana, who are also known as the Tswana. The name *Botswana* means "Land of the Tswana."

The Batswana are made up of several groups. The largest of these groups are the Bangwato, the Bakwena, and the Bangwaketse. Seretse Khama was a member of the Bangwato. The second president of Botswana, Ketumile Masire, belonged to the Bangwaketse group.

Farming and raising cattle are important to the Batswana. A person's wealth is determined by the number of cattle the person owns. Owning cattle is like having money in the bank, because the animals can always be sold or exchanged for necessities.

The kgotla, or meeting place, is usually in the center of a village. *Kgotla* means "court" in Setswana.

The Batswana build large villages that have a rigid structure. The kgosi and his family live in the center of the village. The location of a person's home is determined by his or her relationship to the kgosi. Relatives of the kgosi live closest to the center. People who are not related to the kgosi or who are not Batswana may live on the edge of the village. If outsiders

Botswana's Troubled Neighbor

In recent years, Botswana has had problems with illegal immigrants from Zimbabwe. The problem became more intense in 2000, when the Zimbabwean government began seizing privately owned farmland. By 2005, the Zimbabwean government had taken control of all the valuable farmland in its nation. Hundreds of thousands of Zimbabweans lost their livelihood. Many flooded across the border into Botswana.

By early 2004, an estimated one hundred thousand Zimbabweans had entered Botswana illegally. This number swelled to perhaps two hundred thousand by the end of the year.

To try to stem the tide of illegal immigrants, the Botswana government increased punishment for people who break immigration laws. The Botswana government also built a fence along part of the border. Though Botswana is sending illegal immigrants back to Zimbabwe, many others make their way into Botswana every week. This ongoing problem has strained relations between Botswana and Zimbabwe.

want to live in or near a village, they must ask the kgosi for permission. An outside person may lease land or rent a house in the tribal area that the kgosi approves.

The San

No ethnic group has been in Botswana longer than the San. The San once lived in all of southern Africa. Today, they live in remote areas of Botswana, Namibia, Angola, South Africa, Zimbabwe, and Zambia. When white settlers first arrived in Africa, they considered the San a threat because the San occasionally killed the settlers' livestock. The settlers killed many San.

A San family walking across the grasslands. Some San still live their traditional way, hunting and gathering food for their survival.

A San hunter takes aim. The San traditionally tipped their arrows with poison.

The San are made up of a number of groups. Each group has its own language. San languages sound like a series of clicks. When writing a San language, slashes and exclamation marks are used to show where there are clicks.

Traditionally, the San were nomadic people. They lived in small bands of related families. Their homes were temporary circular huts made from branches and grass. The San carried few possessions with them. They owned little beyond bows and poison-tipped arrows, simple clothing, and musical instruments. These San moved constantly, searching for food. San men were the hunters. Women were the gatherers. They used a wooden stick to dig up roots and bulbs. The women also collected seeds, berries, fruits, and caterpillars to eat.

The San were also known as excellent animal trackers. To the untrained eye, their skills were almost magical. But to the San, tracking an animal was as simple as reading a book. The Kalahari was their book. By looking at the clues an animal left behind, the San could tell the animal's age and sex.

Living in the Kalahari Desert, the San became skilled at finding water. Sometimes they would get water from melons or other plants with thick underground stems. The San also used ostrich eggs to hold water. Today, finding water is not as hard as it once was. The government of Botswana has drilled many boreholes around the country. These long, narrow shafts go deep into the earth to pump up fresh water, even in the driest areas.

In the 1990s, the Botswana government began strongly encouraging the San to leave their traditional homeland, the Central Kalahari Game Reserve. The San were relocated to a settlement outside of the Kalahari. Because of this, the San are losing their ancient traditions. Some have forgotten how to track, hunt, and survive under harsh desert conditions. Many now live in permanent homes and receive food from the government. In 2006, a court ruled that the San have the right to live in the Central Kalahari Game Reserve. Some are committed to returning to the desert, but many others will remain in villages.

The Peoples of Botswana

Batswana	79%
Kalanga	11%
San	3%
Kgalagadi, white, and others	7%

The Khoikhoi are an ethnic group similar to the San. Like the San, the Khoikhoi speak a "clicking" language. Traditionally, the Khoikhoi were more settled than the San, and some kept large herds of sheep and cattle.

The Kalanga are the largest ethnic group in Botswana after the Batswana. During colonial times, the borders drawn between countries were sometimes totally random. The European powers drawing the borders paid no attention to where the various ethnic groups lived. As a result, the Kalanga found themselves split between two countries, which are now Zimbabwe and Botswana. Today, most Kalanga live in Zimbabwe, while the rest live in northeastern Botswana.

The Kalanga have different ways of life from the Batswana. Instead of forming large villages, they live in small family groups. Owning livestock does not determine wealth or status. Instead, owning land increases power and wealth. To the Kalanga, marriage is an important way for a family to gain more land.

The Herero people live in both Namibia and Botswana. Herero women are easy to identify. They wear long cotton dresses designed with many colors and patterns. They also wear a cotton wrap around their head. This style of clothing dates back to the 1800s. When German missionaries first came to southern Africa, their wives encouraged the Herero women to dress as they did. The Herero accepted the Germans' advice and continue to dress this way today.

Botswana has a small white population. Some of them were born in Botswana and are considered citizens. In recent

years, however, some white workers have been immigrating to Botswana. Many are from South Africa or the Balkan region of southeastern Europe. Some Chinese people have also immigrated to Botswana. Cultural differences have sometimes made tensions flare between the citizens of Botswana and these new immigrants.

A woman in typical Herero clothing. The headdress is styled after that of the German missionaries who worked among the Herero in the 1800s.

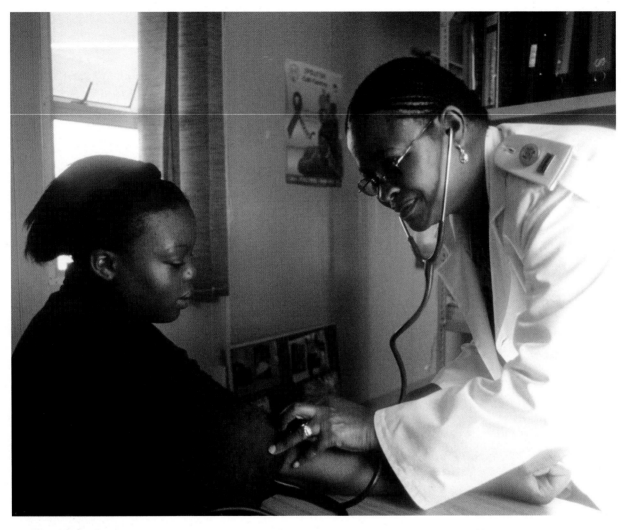

Dr. Niomi Seboni, a teacher at the University of Botswana, checks a girl's blood pressure.

Health Care

After Botswana became independent, the new government began a program to deal with the nation's health problems. This program was based on the idea of decreasing poverty in order to improve health. The program worked, and Botswana became one of the healthiest countries in southern Africa.

In recent years, however, Botswana has faced a huge health crisis. AIDS, a deadly disease caused by the HIV virus, has devastated the country. In the early 1990s, a person in Botswana could expect to live an average of sixty years. Today, because of the terrible toll of AIDS, the average life expectancy in Botswana has plummeted to just thirty-four years. It is estimated that about one in four adults in Botswana is infected with HIV. Many people not infected also pay a terrible price. Botswana has more than 120,000 orphans because of HIV/AIDS.

Botswana has the world's second-highest rate of adults with HIV/AIDS. Only Swaziland has a higher percentage of adults with the virus.

Setswana Numbers

nngwe fêla	one
pedi	two
tharo	three
nnê	four
tlhano	five
thataro	six
supa	seven
bofêra bobedi	eight
bofêra bongwe	nine
lesomê	ten

The government of Botswana is working hard to deal with this crisis. When AIDS first became widespread in the 1980s, there was no known treatment. Though scientists still have not found a cure, in the late 1990s, they discovered medicines that can control the disease. In many poor countries around the world, people cannot afford these medicines. But in 2002, the Botswana government began trying to provide the drugs free of charge to everyone who needs them. By 2004, about half the people who needed the medicine were getting it.

The government is also trying to prevent the spread of the disease. In the past, many people did not want to be tested for HIV. They were embarrassed, because HIV is often spread through sexual contact. Now, HIV testing is part of regular checkups in clinics and hospitals across the country. Making it a routine test has helped reduce the shame attached to it. Botswana is also working to educate people about how to prevent the spread of HIV/AIDS. Children are taught about the disease from the time they are in primary school. Though HIV/AIDS remains a huge problem in Botswana, the country's efforts to combat it are a model for other nations.

Common Setswana Words and Phrases

Yes	*Ee*
No	*Nnyaa*
Hello; good morning; good afternoon; good evening	*Dumela*
How are you?	*Le kae?*
I am fine.	*Ke tsogile sentle.*
Thank you	*Ke itumetse*
How much is this?	*Ke bo kae?*

Language

Two major languages are spoken in Botswana: English, the official language used in business and legal affairs, and Setswana, the national language. The two languages are extremely different.

In English, a word has the same meaning whether it is said with a high voice pitch or a low pitch. In Setswana, a word can have several different meanings depending on the pitch. For example, "Ke motho" can mean "I am a person" or "It is a person" depending on the speaker's pitch.

Many people in Botswana speak both Setswana and English. Signs are often in both languages.

Education

Children in Botswana are not legally required to go to school. Still, most do. In 2001, 84 percent of children were enrolled in primary school. The nation's primary schools are free. Children begin school between the ages of six and ten and continue for up to seven years. The Botswana government is committed to improving schools. In 2005, 26 percent of government spending was dedicated to education. The government wants to

More than 80 percent of children in Botswana attend elementary school.

develop an educated workforce in Botswana. The hope is that education will provide Botswana with more skilled workers in the technology field.

Classes in Botswana tend to be large. Each teacher generally has between twenty-eight and thirty-eight students. When funds get low, teachers sometimes buy supplies for the school. In the afternoon, lunches are served at school. In a village, the school kitchen may be nothing more than huge boiling pots of beans and mealie meale cooking over fires on a concrete slab. Children must wear uniforms to school. If a child is from a poor family, the government will provide uniforms and food.

Most subjects are taught in English. Topics covered in the fifth grade include math, cultural studies such as values and taboos, Setswana, health education (the main topic is AIDS), and performing arts like dancing and singing.

Secondary school begins at age thirteen and lasts for five years. In 2001, about 59 percent of children in Botswana went on to secondary school.

Some students who finish secondary school go on to university. The nation's largest university is the University of Botswana. In 2004, the university had about fifteen thousand students. Other students go on to higher education at the Institutes of Health Sciences and Ba Isago University College.

Botswana also has many technical and vocational training centers. This includes teacher-training colleges and an agricultural college.

Secondary school in Botswana is divided into two parts, junior secondary school and senior secondary school. Most senior secondary schools have computer labs.

Spiritual Life

92

${B}$OTSWANA'S CONSTITUTION GUARANTEES FREEDOM OF religion for all citizens. About half the people of Botswana are Christian, yet many of them continue to hold some traditional beliefs.

Opposite: **The London Missionary Society Church in Serowe was built in 1912.**

People leave church in Serowe after a Sunday morning service.

Botswana's Traditional Doctors

Traditional doctors called *dingaka* (one doctor is a *ngaka*) are central to traditional beliefs in Botswana. A ngaka can have many different skills. He or she might predict future events. He might specialize in rainmaking. He might cure the sick. Some dingaka have all these skills, while others have just one.

Dingaka use herbs, leaves, bark, and roots to heal the sick. Many people in Botswana trust them to cure snakebites, get rid of pain, and cure the flu.

To tell the future, dingaka use divining dice or divining bones. A ngaka throws the dice or bones and then interprets their position. This ritual may be used to answer questions big and small, from ""Why hasn't there been rain?" to "What kind of car should I buy?"

To become a ngaka, a person must serve as an apprentice under an experienced ngaka for two or three years. The apprentice usually pays the ngaka one cow for the apprenticeship.

Dingaka dress differently than other people in Botswana, so they're easy to identify. A ngaka's outfit might consist of a jackal-skin hat and a necklace made from the backbone of a snake. Around his neck, he might also have containers filled with medicines. A ngaka may carry a cow horn filled with charms, the jaw of a monitor lizard, or the horn of a dikdik, a small antelope.

In Botswana, all practicing dingaka must register with the Botswana Dingaka Association. This association holds conferences to discuss issues and provide educational talks.

Traditional Religions

Ancestors play a large role in Botswana's traditional religions. Most people in Botswana, even if they are Christian, acknowledge the power and influence of ancestors in their daily lives. They believe it is important to act in a way that respects and pleases their ancestors.

The Batswana's name for the highest god is Modimo. The plural is Badimo, which means "ancestor." Badimo is also the name of the Batswana's traditional religion.

The various groups that comprise the Batswana have different creation stories. But all the groups agree that the first ancestors emerged from the ground via sacred caves.

Huge footprints can be seen in the stone in the area where the Bakgatla people live. The Bakgatla say that a Matsieng, or giant ancestor, led people and animals up from the middle of Earth. In the beginning, the outside of Earth was soft, so the Matsieng left footprints on the rock. Other prehistoric footprints have been found elsewhere in Botswana. They are also said to have come from ancient ancestors.

According to the San, in the distant past everything could talk. Plants could talk, animals could talk. Even rocks and trees and the wind could talk. At one point, however, all these things stopped talking. But, since all things could once talk, everything in the world is connected.

The San believe that bad events happen because of something they or someone else did. They sometimes use dance to change bad fortune. To do this, woman sing while men dance in a way that sends them into a trance. The San believe that

Religions of Botswana (2001)

Christian	71.6%
Badimo (traditional religion)	6%
Other	1.4%
None or unspecified	21%

people in a trance have healing power. This power can be used to help someone overcome sickness, to bring rain, or to change any other misfortune that has happened.

Early Christian Missionaries

Christianity was introduced to the area that is now Botswana by explorers in the nineteenth century. Some of these explorers were missionaries who came to Africa in the hope of converting people to Christianity.

David Livingstone, one of the region's most famous missionaries, arrived in 1841. He established a mission station among the Bakwena. Livingstone was more interested in exploring Africa than in his missionary work. He was one of the first Europeans to travel across the entire continent. Still, by the middle of the nineteenth century, he was having some success in his missionary work. He convinced a leader of the Bakwena, Kgosi Sechele I, to become Christian.

Many local chiefs encouraged missionaries to settle in their villages. One reason was that traders were more likely to visit villages that had missionaries. Another reason was that missionaries carried guns, which were valuable to the tribes. Christianity spread quickly in Botswana. By 1880, every tribe had missionaries living among them.

Christianity Today

The main Christian churches in Botswana today are Roman Catholic, Anglican, Methodist, United Congregational

Church of Southern Africa, and Zion Christian. Botswana is also home to a number of Lutherans, Baptists, Jehovah's Witnesses, and members of the Church of Jesus Christ of Latter-day Saints, who are often called Mormons. Missionaries still come to Botswana from foreign lands. Missionary groups in Botswana today include Mormons, Quakers, Baptists, Lutherans, and Mennonites.

Missionaries first came to Botswana in the early 1800s. The percentage of Christians in Botswana has been increasing ever since.

Dancing is important in the Zion
Christian Church. Members sometimes leap high into the air and
then come hard onto the ground,
symbolically stamping on evil.

Many churches in Botswana combine Christian beliefs and ceremonies with traditional African beliefs and practices. Members of the Zion Christian Church believe in faith healing. They also believe that high officials in the church can communicate with their ancestors. People belonging to the Zion Christian Church can be identified by the badge they wear. This badge consists of a metal star or dove on a black circle against a rectangular green background.

Botswana's Religious Holidays

Good Friday	March or April
Easter	March or April
Easter Monday	March or April
Ascension Day	May or June
Christmas	December 25

Other Religions

Botswana has about five thousand followers of Islam. Most trace their heritage back to South Asia. About three thousand Hindus also live in Botswana.

Botswana is home to a small community of people who follow the Baha'i faith. This religion teaches that mankind should be unified across the globe. The Baha'i believe that God creates certain events that break down barriers between races, classes, and nations. People will be unified once all those events have occurred.

Arts and
Sports

THE OLDEST EVIDENCE OF ART IN BOTSWANA DATES BACK thousands of years. Rock paintings abound in the Tsodilo Hills of northwestern Botswana. Today, singing, dancing, and storytelling are vital parts of the culture. Traditional song and dance performances are a part of every public holiday celebration.

Opposite: **A wooden carving in the Okavango Delta**

Children gather around a fire to watch a traditional San dance.

Music and Dance

Music is an everyday part of life in Botswana. It can be heard while shopping, while visiting a school, or while driving. Churches are often filled with song. Church music includes both Western Christian songs and traditional African music.

Children are taught to sing and dance in school. School assemblies often begin with singing. Many schoolchildren also take part in dance competitions. At the competitions, they wear traditional outfits made of animal skins and beads. They also wear ankle rattles. The dances tend to be quite energetic.

San schoolchildren perform a healing dance. In traditional San culture, healing dances lasted all night.

Many traditional songs in Botswana have a call-and-response pattern. One person or group will sing some words, and then a second group answers. The lyrics often repeat. Songs usually end with the singers letting out a loud, high wail. Traditional dancers sing and clap while dancing. Female dancers often use exaggerated hip movements and facial expressions.

Some traditional dances have spiritual purposes. The Kalanga, for instance, have a dance that is supposed to bring rain. Another dance is performed to heal the sick.

Dancing is central to San culture.

A San man plays a traditional instrument.

The San have their own dances and music. One of their most common musical instruments is made from a curved stick or bow with one string. The musician sits on the ground to play this instrument. One end of the bow rests on a metal pan on the ground. Plucking the string in different places produces a variety of sounds.

The Ostrich Mating Dance Game is a San dance. One main dancer stands in the center. The women sit on the ground while the men form a line. Each group claps and sings. The men stomp their feet in the loose dirt while waiting for their turn to dance with the center dancer. When dancing, they may roll and tumble in the dirt. Sometimes they jump and kick a leg over the center dancer's head.

Women watch while men perform the Ostrich Mating Dance Game.

The Mogwana Dance Troupe

The Mogwana Dance Troupe was formed in 1991 to promote traditional dance and music. Its members perform traditional dances from Botswana and elsewhere in southern Africa. The Mogwana troupe takes its name from a type of nut. "You cannot break the Mogwana nut," says the group's leader, Gaolape Basuhi. "It is unbreakable, and we are determined to be unbreakable in trying to promote Botswana culture through dance."

The troupe has thrilled audiences all around the world. The Mogwana dancers also run workshops to teach the dances to other troupes. In this way, they are ensuring that Botswana's traditional culture will not die.

Crafts

Many traditional crafts are thriving in Botswana. People have long used palm fronds to make watertight baskets. The palm fiber is dyed and woven into intricate patterns. These baskets are both beautiful and useful. These can be used to store grain or other goods or to carry water. Because of the fine quality of baskets made in Botswana, they are sold in North America, Europe, Australia, and other parts of Africa.

Bayei women of north-western Botswana weave reeds into baskets. Bayei baskets are known for their geometric designs.

A hunter carves a design onto an ostrich eggshell, which he will use to carry water. The design is used to identify the shell's owner.

Another popular craft in Botswana is decorating ostrich eggshells. The San carve intricate designs on the outside of the shells. Pieces of these shells are made into beads that are strung into necklaces, bracelets, and earrings.

Craftspeople use wood to make bowls, spoons, and bangles. Some highly skilled carpenters make the kgotla chair, a folding wooden chair. Carving human and animal figures from wood is also popular.

The First Elephant

People everywhere tell stories. In Botswana, many traditional stories relate how different creatures were created.

One story describes how the first elephant was made. The story begins with a young woman and her baby. The woman could not leave her tent, because in Botswana new mothers are supposed to stay inside for three months to protect their babies from harm. This woman was sad because her husband did not bring her enough food. She was crying one day when a flat basket—called a *leselo*—appeared. This type of basket was used to separate the husks from grain. The woman heard the voices of her ancestors urging her to step on the basket. She agreed and stepped onto the leselo. Slowly, she and her baby merged and were transformed into an elephant.

Stories such as this show the close relationship between elephants and the people of Botswana. Most people in Botswana will not eat elephant meat. They consider elephants their cousins.

Decorative weavings do not have a long history in Botswana. But over the years, a group of weavers has gathered in the small village of Oodi, just north of Gaborone. These weavers make tablecloths, wall hangings, jackets, bedspreads, and pillow covers out of sheep's wool that has been hand-dyed and hand-spun. Some of the textiles have a village scene or animal design woven into them.

Pottery was first made in the region that is now Botswana thousands of years ago. Some pottery is still made in Botswana

Many tourists who visit Botswana return home with textiles or carvings as souvenirs.

today. Gray clay is collected from rivers and then shaped into pots. After the pots are fired, they are painted with brightly colored designs.

Botswana has a huge cattle population, so leatherwork is an important craft. Sturdy sandals and bags are made from leather. The skins of animals such as goats are sometimes made into rugs. The skins of wild animals such as zebras are also used to make rugs or other items, but the government tries to control this.

A woman lays out leather sandals for sale on a sidewalk in Gabarone.

The National Museum and Art Gallery

The National Museum and Art Gallery is located in the middle of Gaborone. It displays traditional crafts and the work of current Botswana artists. Every year, the gallery hosts several exhibitions to promote the work of local artists. It is considered one of the top galleries in southern Africa.

Education is central to the museum's purpose. It displays items from Botswana's history, such as a traditional hut and old carts and other vehicles.

The museum also has a mobile service that brings art and artifacts to people living outside of the city of Gaborone.

Seabo Gabanakgosi (number 15) of Botswana's national soccer team fights Morocco's Youssef Mokhtari for the ball in a game in 2005.

Sports

Softball, volleyball, and tennis are all popular sports in Botswana. But the country's favorite sport is soccer. The national team is called the Zebras. Fans go wild when their Zebras play another country's team at the National Stadium.

Cricket is a bat-and-ball game that was brought to Botswana by immigrants from South Africa and South Asia. Botswana joined the International Cricket Council in 2001, and the sport is growing more popular among young people. Most cricket matches take place in and around the capital city, Gaborone.

Botswana has also sent athletes to the Olympics. So far, none has won a medal.

Botswana's Glody Duby (far right) competed in the 800-meter race at the 2004 Olympics.

Life in Botswana

For many people in Botswana, the village is the center of life. Villages can be very different from one another. Some villages are mainly agricultural. People in them grow food or raise cattle. Other villages grew up around mines where most of the men work. Villages have also grown up near game parks. The people in these villages work in the tourist industry.

Opposite: **A smiling child in Botswana**

This traditional thatched building is now a tourist shop.

Housing

Most urban homes in Botswana are simple and modern. They are made of concrete block and stucco. In the newer neighborhoods, many homes have been built with the help of the Self Help Housing Agency. By helping people build quality housing, this agency is trying to prevent the growth of the ramshackle slums that sometimes grow in poor areas.

Workers in Gabarone lay down a cement floor. Most new houses in Botswana are basic and sturdy.

Village housing is quite different from that found in cities like Gaborone or Francistown. Many people who live in villages live in a traditional home called a *rondavel*. Rondavels are usually circular. The walls are made of mud and cow dung. The roof is supported with beams. On top of the beams is a thick layer of straw that comes to a pointed top. Women are responsible for building the rondavels.

Rondavels are simple rural houses. The roofs are usually held up with tree branches.

A San rests outside his flat.

Some people in Botswana believe that living in a rondavel is a sign of poverty. They prefer to live in rectangular homes with flat roofs. These homes are called flats.

People who live in villages but work in the city often have a home in both places. In rural areas, people sometimes move among three different places. One is a village home near shops and schools. The second is in an area called "the lands," which is outside the village. This is where crops are grown and tended. The third is the cattle post. This is a spot far from the village where cattle are kept. Younger boys and older men often live at the cattle post, keeping watch over

Beliefs About Babies

After a woman gives birth, she and her baby must live separately from everyone else for three months. During this time, the mother is waited on and helped. An old superstition says that if this does not happen, the baby will become a bed wetter or will grow up dull and thickheaded.

the family's livestock. The men at the cattle post live in a rondavel. A stick fence built around the rondavel is used to corral the cattle.

Living in a Village

Privacy is rare for people who live in villages. Gossip spreads quickly, and everyone seems to know what everybody else is doing. Problems that concern the village are dealt with in the kgotla.

Women rest by their hut in a settlement outside the Central Kalahari Game Reserve.

In rural areas, life can be very quiet. The ring of cowbells is one of the most common sounds. Even in larger villages like Serowe, cowbells echo through the valley.

Shopping can be a challenge in rural villages. When a shop runs out of an item, it is gone. Sometimes, another shop in the village will carry the same item. But more likely, you have to wait until the delivery truck arrives. Rural villages tend to be sleepy places, so the arrival of the truck is a highlight. It brings a buzz of activity. People crowd around the truck and even help the driver unload!

Gabarone is home to several Western-style shopping malls.

Village shops can be extremely simple. A barbershop, for instance, might be a hut with a plastic chair for customers. A sign reading "Barber" is taped outside.

Garbage is a common problem in many villages. Most have no garbage pickup. Instead, people make piles of garbage and then burn them. Garbage is commonly seen alongside of roads.

Many people in Botswana use cars, but in the countryside, donkey carts are common. Some carts carry large plastic bins filled with food for sale.

In the countryside, many people use donkey carts to haul goods.

Food Vocabulary

borôthô	bread
metsi	water
nama	meat
mashi	milk
loungô	fruit
dinotshe	honey

Food

A grain called sorghum is a staple in the diet of the people of Botswana. Cornmeal is also a staple. It is usually called mealie meal or maize. Today, people eat more maize than sorghum. One reason for this is that maize is usually available in stores, while sorghum is not. People often have to grind the sorghum at home themselves.

One of the main ways of preparing either sorghum or maize is to mix it with boiling water. The mixture is stirred until it makes a soft paste. Then it is cooked. Ingredients can be added to the cooked maize or sorghum. A popular breakfast dish called *ting* is made by adding milk and sugar. The result is a type of porridge. Ting can also be turned into a lunch or dinner by adding meat and vegetables.

Meat is readily available in Botswana. Beef is popular, particularly at ceremonies like weddings. Chicken, lamb, mutton, and goat are also common. Some people also eat wild game. Some types of antelope are especially popular. Kudu sausage might be served for breakfast, or oryx fillet for dinner.

People in Botswana prepare meat in many different ways. Beef can be barbecued or sun-dried to make a quick snack. For important ceremonies, *seswaa* is sometimes prepared. Seswaa is made in a three-legged pot. Often, only water and salt are added to flavor the meat. Another meat dish is *serobe*. It is made from the intestines of a cow, sheep, or goat.

Many fruits and vegetables are grown in Botswana. Common vegetables include cabbage, onions, tomatoes, lettuce, peas, beans, and spinach. Watermelons and other types of melons are also harvested.

Making Seswaa

Here's a recipe for seswaa, a popular dish made of pounded meat.

Ingredients

2½ lbs. beef brisket

water to cover meat

1 large onion, chopped

salt to taste

pepper to taste

Directions

Place the beef, onion, salt, and pepper in a saucepan. Cover with water and cook over medium heat for about two and a half hours until soft.

Drain the liquid and remove the bones. Pound the meat until it is flaky. Serve with mealie meal and cabbage.

Social Customs

People in Botswana have a different way of shaking hands than people in North America. When shaking hands, you extend one hand and place your other hand on your wrist. You also extend both hands when handing someone something. This tradition may date back to tribal times. Showing both hands lets the person see that you were not holding a weapon.

Similarly, when someone accepts a gift, they use both hands. This is done instead of saying the words "thank you."

People in Botswana always greet each other when they approach. Each stops and says hello and asks how the other is doing. It is considered rude to not stop and talk. Men and women are addressed differently in Botswana. The polite way to address a man is by calling him *Rra*. Women are called *Mma*.

Diketlo

Diketlo is a Botswanan game that is lot like jacks. To play it, draw a circle on the ground. Put ten stones in the circle. The first player starts by throwing a rock into the air. She then scoops all the rocks out of the circle before catching the thrown rock. The player throws the rock into the air again. This time, she grabs one rock and puts it in the center of the circle before catching the thrown rock. Again, the player throws the rock into the air. This time, she scoops two rocks into the circle. The first player's turn continues with her grabbing an additional rock each time. If she misses a rock or doesn't catch the rock that was thrown in the air, it is the next player's turn. She starts at the beginning, with ten rocks inside the circle.

Death and Burial in Botswana

In the past, the death ceremony in Botswana was simple. Relatives would share food at the home of the dead person. The burial took place on the day of the death.

Today, the death ceremony is more complicated and expensive. People gather at the dead person's home for one week. During that time, they pray and eat. No one brings food. Instead, the dead person's relatives provide food for all of the visitors. This usually involves killing a cow or two. As many as two hundred people may visit the home. Sometimes, complete strangers even show up for a free meal.

Buying the most beautiful, expensive coffin is also considered important. In some areas, a canvas roof attached to poles is placed over the grave site. This keeps the grave from getting rained on.

Getting Along

The basic social structure in Botswana is based on two Setswana words: *botho* and *morero*. *Botho* means "to have good qualities." Qualities that are valued include compassion, politeness, helpfulness, consideration for others, and respect for older people. If a person does not have these qualities, he or she is not considered a good person.

Morero means "to consult with others." In Botswana, morero is important within the family, within the community, and in the national government. It is not uncommon for the president to ask average people in Botswana what they think about different issues. Morero is the way the people of Botswana reach agreements and follow through on decisions.

Over the years, the idea of morero has been a boon to the people of Botswana. It has helped them live in peace and harmony, as one united people.

Cooperation and helping others are among the most important values taught in Botswana.

Timeline

Botswana History		World History	
People live in the area that is now Botswana.	100,000 years ago		
		2500 B.C.	Egyptians build the pyramids and the Sphinx in Giza.
		563 B.C.	The Buddha is born in India.
People begin keeping cattle in northern Botswana.	ca. 300 B.C.		
Iron smelting begins in the Tswapong Hills near Palapye.	A.D. 190		
		A.D. 313	The Roman emperor Constantine legalizes Christianity.
Farming settlements are established near the Okavango Delta.	550		
		610	The Prophet Muhammad begins preaching a new religion called Islam.
The Batswana migrate to eastern Botswana, pushing the San into the Kalahari Desert.	ca. 1000		
		1054	The Eastern (Orthodox) and Western (Roman Catholic) Churches break apart.
		1095	The Crusades begin.
		1215	King John seals the Magna Carta.
		1300s	The Renaissance begins in Italy.
		1347	The plague sweeps through Europe.
		1453	Ottoman Turks capture Constantinople, conquering the Byzantine Empire.
		1492	Columbus arrives in North America.
		1500s	Reformers break away from the Catholic Church, and Protestantism is born.
		1776	The U.S. Declaration of Independence is signed.
		1789	The French Revolution begins.
Missionary David Livingstone arrives in southern Africa.	1841		

Botswana History

Dutch South Africans raid the area of Botswana.	1852
Gold is discovered.	1867
The British establish the Bechuanaland Protectorate.	1885
The British impose a hut tax on Bechuanaland.	1899
Bangwato chief Seretse Khama marries a white Englishwoman, causing a furor in southern Africa.	1948
Seretse Khama is forced to leave Bechuanaland.	1950
Seretse Khama renounces his chieftainship and is allowed to return to Bechuanaland.	1956
The Central Kalahari Game Reserve is established as a homeland for the San.	1961
Botswana gains independence; Seretse Khama becomes the first president.	1966
Diamonds are discovered near Letlhakane.	1967
The pula is introduced as the new national currency.	1976
Seretse Khama dies; Vice President Ketumile Masire becomes president.	1980
South African troops raid Botswana.	1985–1986
The Botswana government begins removing the San from the Central Kalahari Game Reserve.	1990s
Festus Mogae becomes president.	1998
A court ruling affirms the San's right to live in the Central Kalahari Game Reserve.	2006

World History

1865	The American Civil War ends.
1879	The first practical light bulb is invented.
1914	World War I begins.
1917	The Bolshevik Revolution brings communism to Russia.
1929	A worldwide economic depression begins.
1939	World War II begins.
1945	World War II ends.
1957	The Vietnam War begins.
1969	Humans land on the Moon.
1975	The Vietnam War ends.
1989	The Berlin Wall is torn down as communism crumbles in Eastern Europe.
1991	The Soviet Union breaks into separate states.
2001	Terrorists attack the World Trade Center in New York City and the Pentagon in Washington, D.C.

Fast Facts

Official name: Republic of Botswana

Capital: Gaborone

Official language: English

Serowe

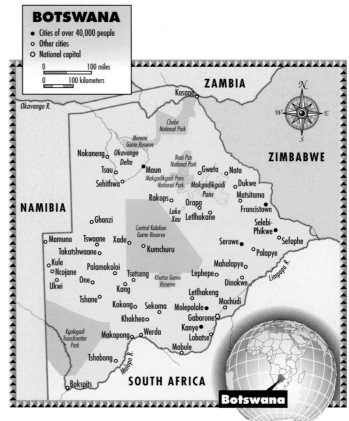

BOTSWANA
- Cities of over 40,000 people
- Other cities
- National capital

0   100 miles
0   100 kilometers

ZAMBIA

Okavango R.

Kasane

Chobe National Park

Moremi Game Reserve

ZIMBABWE

Nokaneng   Okavango Delta

Nxai Pan National Park

Tsau   Maun   Gweta   Nata

Sehithwa   Makgadikgadi Pans National Park   Makgadikgadi Pans   Dukwe

Matsitama

Rakops   Orapa   Francistown

NAMIBIA   Lake Xau   Letlhakane   Selebi-Phikwe

Ghanzi   Central Kalahari Game Reserve   Serowe   Sefophe

Mamuno   Tswagne   Xade   Palapye

Takatshwaane   Kumchuru   Mahalapye

Kule   Palamakoloi   Tsetseng   Khutse Game Reserve   Lephepe   Dinokwe

Ncojane   One   Letlhakeng   Mochudi

Ukwi   Kang   Kokong   Sekoma   Molepolole

Tshane   Khakhea   Gaborone

Kgalagadi Transfrontier Park   Makopong   Werda   Kanye   Lobatse

Mabule

Tshabong   Limpopo R.

Molopo R.

Bokspits   SOUTH AFRICA

Botswana

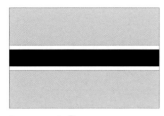

Botswana's flag

Baobab tree

Official religion:	None
Founding date:	September 30, 1966
National anthem:	"Fatshe Leno La Rona" ("Blessed Be This Noble Land")
Government:	Multiparty republic
Chief of state:	President
Area:	224,607 square miles (581,730 sq km)
Greatest distance north to south:	625 miles (1,006 km)
Greatest distance east to west:	590 miles (950 km)
Bordering countries:	Namibia to the west, Zambia to the west and north, Zimbabwe to the northeast, and South Africa to the southeast and south
Highest elevation:	Otse Mountain, 4,886 feet (1,489 m)
Lowest elevation:	Where the Shashe and Limpopo rivers meet, 1,684 feet (513 m)
Average temperature:	100°F (38°C) in January; 32°F (0°C) in July
Lowest annual rainfall:	5 inches (13 cm), in the west
Highest annual rainfall:	25 inches (64 cm), in the north
National population (2006 est.):	1,639,833

The National Museum
and Art Gallery

Currency

**Population of largest
cities and villages
(2001 est.):**

Gaborone	186,007
Francistown	83,023
Molepolole	54,561
Selebi-Phikwe	49,849
Maun	43,776
Serowe	42,444

Famous landmarks:
- ▶ *National Museum and Art Gallery*, Gaborone
- ▶ *Tsodilo Hills*, northwestern Kalahari Desert
- ▶ *Chobe National Park*, northern Botswana
- ▶ *Moremi Game Reserve*, Okavango Delta
- ▶ *Kgosi Sechele I Museum*, Molepolole
- ▶ *Makgadikgadi Pans National Park*, Maun

Industry: Botswana is the largest diamond producer in the world. Diamonds account for about 80 percent of Botswana's exports. Tourism is also central to the economy. In 2002, more than one million visitors spent more than US$300 million. Cattle are Botswana's most important agricultural product. In 2003, there were 1,700,000 head of cattle in the country.

Currency: The pula is the basic unit of currency. In 2007, about 6 pula was equal to US$1.

Weights and measures: Metric system

Literacy rate: 81%

Schoolchildren

Seretse Khama

Common Setswana words and phrases:

Ee	Yes
Nnyaa	No
Dumela	Hello
Le kae?	How are you?
Ke tsogile sentle.	I am fine.
Ke itumetse	Thank you
Ke bo kae?	How much is this?

Famous Botswanans:

Khama III   (ca. 1835–1923)
Kgosi

Seretse Khama   (1921–1980)
First president of Botswana

Tshekedi Khama   (1905–1959)
Regent

Ketumile Masire   (1925–)
President

Festus Mogae   (1939–)
President

To Find Out More

Books

▶ Bolaane, Maitseo, and Part T. Mgadla. *Batswana*. New York: Rosen Publishing Group, 1997.

▶ Freedman, Frances. *David Livingstone*. Milwaukee: World Almanac Library, 2002.

▶ Lewin, Ted, and Betsy Lewin. *Elephant Quest*. New York: HarperCollins, 2000.

▶ Porter, Linda. *The San of Africa*. Minneapolis: Lerner, 2002.

Web Sites

▶ **Botswana Tourism**
http://www.botswana-tourism.gov.bw
For information on Botswana's geography, government, attractions, plants and animals, and more.

▶ **Embassy of Botswana, Japan**
http://www.botswanaembassy.or.jp
To explore Botswana's culture and traditions, wildlife, and many other subjects.

▶ **The Government of Botswana**
http://www.gov.bw/home.html
To learn all about government and business in Botswana.

Embassies and Organizations

▶ **Embassy of the Republic of Botswana**
1531-3 New Hampshire Ave., NW
Washington, DC 20036
202/244-4990
http://www.botswanaembassy.org

Index

Page numbers in *italics* indicate illustrations.

Meet the Author

Sara Louise Kras's love for travel began when she was a little girl. Her mother took their family to many of the United States' amazing national parks. Sara continued this tradition of travel as she got older. She has lived in Zimbabwe, South Africa, and England. In addition, she has explored Australia, Kenya, Thailand, Cambodia, the Maldives, Japan, Costa Rica, Honduras, Mexico, Canada, Denmark, Antigua, Botswana, France, and the Seychelles.

While visiting Botswana, Sara met with museum curators, who discussed ancient and current customs. She visited schools where children taught her their traditional games. She talked with San people about their culture.

Sara's favorite part of Botswana was the animals. Seeing thousands of elephants and Cape buffalo along the shores of the Chobe River was exhilarating. Following a leopard as it prepared for its evening hunt was thrilling.

"I have always been fascinated with other cultures and ways of life," says Sara. "Seeing people live a completely different lifestyle from what I am used to makes me appreciate

what we have. Finding out about these cultures and then telling children about them is one of my favorite things to do. I love to get children excited about the world they live in and to get them curious to find out more."

Sara grew up in Washington State, Texas, and Colorado. She has always loved the outdoors. She enjoys exploring nature and seeing animals in their natural habitat. Sara currently lives in Glendale, California, with her husband, daughter, and cat. She has written many books for children.

Photo Credits

Photographs © 2008:

africanpictures.net: 56 (Karin Duthie/ Illustrative Options)
AfriPics.com: 110 (Daryl Balfour), 34 top (Wendy Dennis)
Alamy Images: 65, 81, 106, 116 (Karin Duthie), 64 (Mark Eveleigh), 24, 115 (Images of Africa Photobank), 43, 77 (Sylvia Cordaiy Photo Library Ltd.), 87 (The Stock Asylum, LLC), 74 (WorldFoto)
AP Images: 112 (Abdeljalil Bounhar), 118, 119 (Jerome Delay), 113 (Anja Niedringhaus), 10 (Obed Zilwa)
Corbis Images: 78 left (Anthony Bannister/Gallo Images), 102 (Louise Gubb), 51, 97, 133 bottom (Hulton-Deutsch Collection), 2, 35, 79, 94, 107, 108, 114 (Peter Johnson), 100 (Wolfgang Kaehler), cover, 6, 42 (Frans Lanting), 120 (Jehad Nga), 70 (David Reed), 44 (Galen Rowell), 72 (Strauss/Curtis)
Getty Images: 53 (Simon Dack), 98 (Peter Essick), 59 (Gianluigi Guercia), 49, 93 (Bert Hardy), 46 (Hulton Archive), 12 (Alexander Joe), 50 (Keystone), 68 (Michele Westmorland), 103 (Art Wolfe)
Images of Africa: 9, 21, 85 (Martin Harvey), 55 (Ian Michler), 82 (Peter & Beverly Pickford), 14 (Chanan Weiss)
Joe Kras: 7 bottom, 16, 19, 20, 22, 25, 33, 36 top, 58 top, 58 bottom, 61, 66, 76, 80, 90, 92, 109, 111, 117, 121, 125, 127, 130 left, 132 bottom, 132 top, 133 top

Jonah Calinawan: 124
Lauré Communications/Jason Lauré: 38, 86, 105
Lonely Planet Images: 15 (Adrian Bailey), 62 (Richard I'Anson)
Magnum Photos/Stuart Franklin: 75, 104
MapQuest.com, Inc.: 60, 131 top
Minden Pictures: 13, 26 (Richard Du Toit), 28, 36 bottom (Michael & Patricia Fogden), 29 (Tony Heald/ npl), 32, 69 (Frans Lanting), 37 (Mark Moffett), 31 (Yva Momatiuk/ John Eastcott), 34 bottom (Francois Savigny/npl), 27 (Robyn Stewart), 30 (Winfried Wisniewski/ Foto Natura)
Panos Pictures/David Reed: 89
Peter Arnold Inc.: 23 (BIOS Courteau Christophe), 91 (Julio Etchart), 39, 131 bottom (Steffen Honzera), 101 (Gerhard Jaegle), 7 top, 41 (LaTerraMagica), 17 (ullstein-Vision Photos)
Reuters: 67 top (Juda Ngwenya), 54 (Joan Sullivan/STR New)
The Granger Collection, New York: 47
The Image Works/Alinari Archives: 8
Wolfgang Kaehler: 123

Maps by XNR Productions, Inc.